Making a Shephe

John Boakes

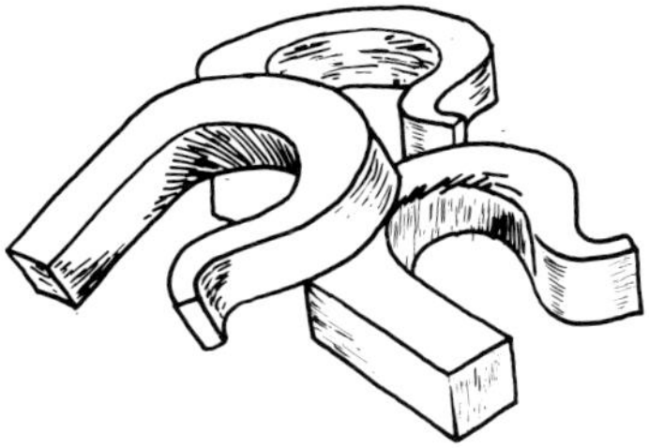

Smith
Settle

First published in 2001 by
Smith Settle Ltd
Ilkley Road
Otley
West Yorkshire
LS21 3JP

ISBN 1 85825 115 X

British Library Cataloguing-in-Publication data:
A catalogue record for this book is available from the British Library.

Set in Monotype Plantin

Designed, printed and bound by
SMITH SETTLE
Ilkley Road, Otley, West Yorkshire LS21 3JP

Introduction

Today stick-making has become an enjoyable hobby. Originally it was a small cottage industry, with people making sticks as they personally needed them. But as their friends and subsequently other people asked for one, their popularity grew, especially those of good stick-makers.

Sticks have been put to many uses over the centuries. Originally they were just used as an aid to working or walking, such as the lonely shepherd working with his crook on the hillside, or the farmer with his thumb-stick to help him as he walked about his farm. They have also been used as a symbol of position and standing. The head of the Church of England, the archbishop of Canterbury, is always to be seen with his ornate staff of office. The long walking stick was even used as a fashion statement: at the end of the seventeenth century, elegant London 'dandies' festooned their long ebonised walking sticks with gaily coloured ribbons as they paraded up and down for all to see.

Of all these uses, the home-made thumb-stick and crook of the farmer and shepherd are perhaps the most important in the evolution of stick-making. The modern-day sticks made for these uses give us a lasting link with the very first sticks ever made. But today the majority of makers do so not for their own use but primarily for enjoyment. Modern-day sticks are not only made at home in the farmhouses and cottages of small villages, but in the flats and semi-detached houses of large towns as well.

It is not possible to say when the first stick or crook was made; perhaps it was from the time when men and trees were first seen on this earth. But it is enough to say that the first shepherd's crook might well have been cut as a length of wood with a branch growing in an inverted 'V' at one end. This crude stick was most probably used in the catching of stock as well as to help walking. From this simple stick came the shepherd's crook, the thumb-stick and the walking stick. These early carved sticks were made during the long winter nights by the light of a flickering candle or smoky paraffin lamp, using only a small sharp knife to carve out the intricate design. It is from these humble beginnings that we now have the beautiful carved sticks that are produced today.

The actual art of stick-making has altered little over the years. The main difference that the passing of time has brought is with the introduction of a larger variety of woods such as cherry, box and plum, and in some cases varieties from abroad. Also, nowadays there is a wider variety of horn available, and this includes buffalo, cow and goat, as well as some of the more unusual breeds of sheep such as Jacob and Lonk in particular.

All around the country it is possible to see a great variety of sticks for sale. These modern ones are normally found in small shops and tobacconists, where they are sold to create an added source of income. Unfortunately, though, from about the middle of this century these have mainly been bought in large quantities from manufacturers in this country and in some cases even from abroad. These factory-made walking sticks and crooks produced in their hundreds are not of the same quality or finish as that of the individually produced stick.

In 1926 the walking-stick industry was centred around Chiddingford, Guildford and Dorking. Around these towns were planted coppices of hazel and chestnut to provide the raw material. The hazel poles were cut every six or seven years, whilst the chestnut, being of a more vigorous nature, were cut every two or three years. The newly cut poles were part-seasoned for a few months before being steam-bent in the factory, and then these newly bent sticks were allowed a few more months to dry out before finally being sold. The factory-made sticks made by this method did not last very long, as they were liable to straighten when wet. But naturally grown bent sticks, on the other hand, were usually made by individual makers and these kept their shape for the lifetime of the stick.

The popularity of stick-dressing today has meant that there are many different classes being competed for at the country fairs and agricultural shows. The best of these home-made sticks are much sought after, and many have even been included in the collections of walking sticks collected by eminent people all over the country. Many of these collections are now open to the public, and one of the best is that which belonged to the late Winston Churchill, now on show at Chartwell in Kent. Over the years, royalty has even shown an interest in the stick-dressers' art; the Queen Mother has a stick that was presented to her by a well-known stick-maker in Thirsk, North Yorkshire.

A lot of the sticks seen at shows and competitions throughout the country are 'craft' or 'carved' sticks. These may be very intricate and beautiful to look at, but they are not really 'working' sticks. A working stick is a tactile object, something the hand wants to hold and in which it feels secure. It must also be strong enough to stand up to a hard day's use out in the fields and hillsides.

One man who makes this sort of stick to the very highest degree is Brian Bannister. Brian lives in the tiny hamlet of Cowgill high up in the Yorkshire Dales, and has been making sticks for well over ten years. During this time he has had several important commissions, including one for a bishop's crozier for the enthronement of the new bishop of Warwick. He has also had over 200 would-be stick-makers of tomorrow through his special one-day introduction courses held in his large workshop situated in the grounds of his home.

The making of a stick is shown in the latter part of this book, as Brian lovingly produces a shepherd's crook. Although today's stick-makers have the benefit of modern-day machines, all the processes are exactly the same as those of the stick-makers of the past.

Bibliography

James Arnold, *The Shell Book of Country Crafts* (1968).
Herbert L Edlin, *Woodland Craft of Britain* (1949 & 1973).
H E Fitzrandolph & M D Hay, *The Rural Industries of England and Wales* (1926 & 1977).
Edward Hart, *Walking Sticks* (1986).
J E Manners, *Country Crafts Today* (1974).
David Morgan Rees, *Yorkshire Craftsmen at Work* (1999).

Acknowledgements

The author would like to thank: stick-maker Brian Bannister and Brian Vie for their help in the writing of this book; and Caroline Benson at the Rural History Centre, Reading University, for permission to reproduce the photographs on pages 8, 10-15.

Some of Brian Bannister's finished sticks.

A bundle of seasoned shafts ready to be used in Brian's Bannister's workshop.

Bundles of freshly cut blackthorn shafts ready for seasoning in the 1940s.

An old-time stick-maker of Linlott & Sons, Surrey, heating the walking sticks in sand so that they can be bent.

The handles are placed in hot sand to set the bend.

Straightening sticks on a *horse* after heating.

Tying a steam-bent handle around an iron ring.

A Welsh stick-maker shaping the handle.

Then finishing a crook in comfort at home.

(Right) Brian Bannister marks out the shape of the handle from a section of seasoned wood. *(Above)* The wood is chosen from Brian's stock.

(Left) Preparing to cut out the shape with a bandsaw. *(Below)* The handle is finally cut out and ready for the next stage.

The shape that is needed for a shepherd's crook.

A box of ready-cut handles waiting to be used. Sometimes it is less wasteful to cut more than one handle from a piece of wood.

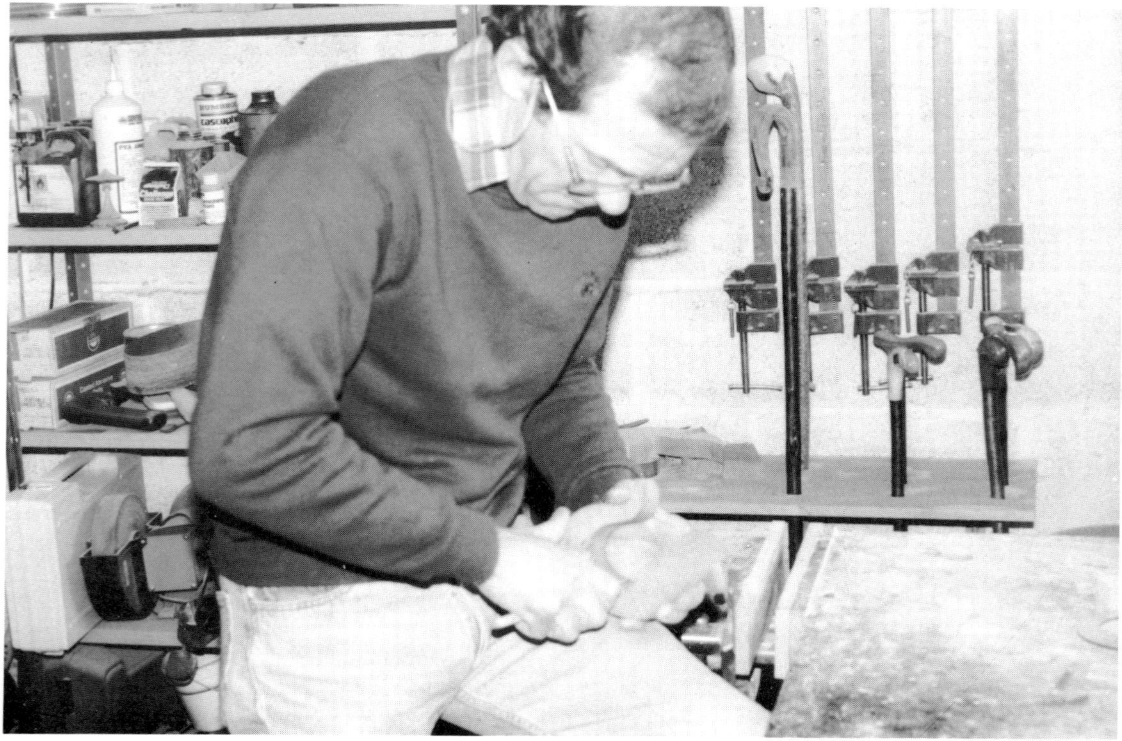

The whittling down of the freshly cut handle to give a more rounded shape and feel.

The inside is whittled away to a rough shape first.

The three different stages of shaping a handle.

Marking out the position on the handle where the metal pin will go to secure the head to the shaft.

Drilling the hole for the metal pin.

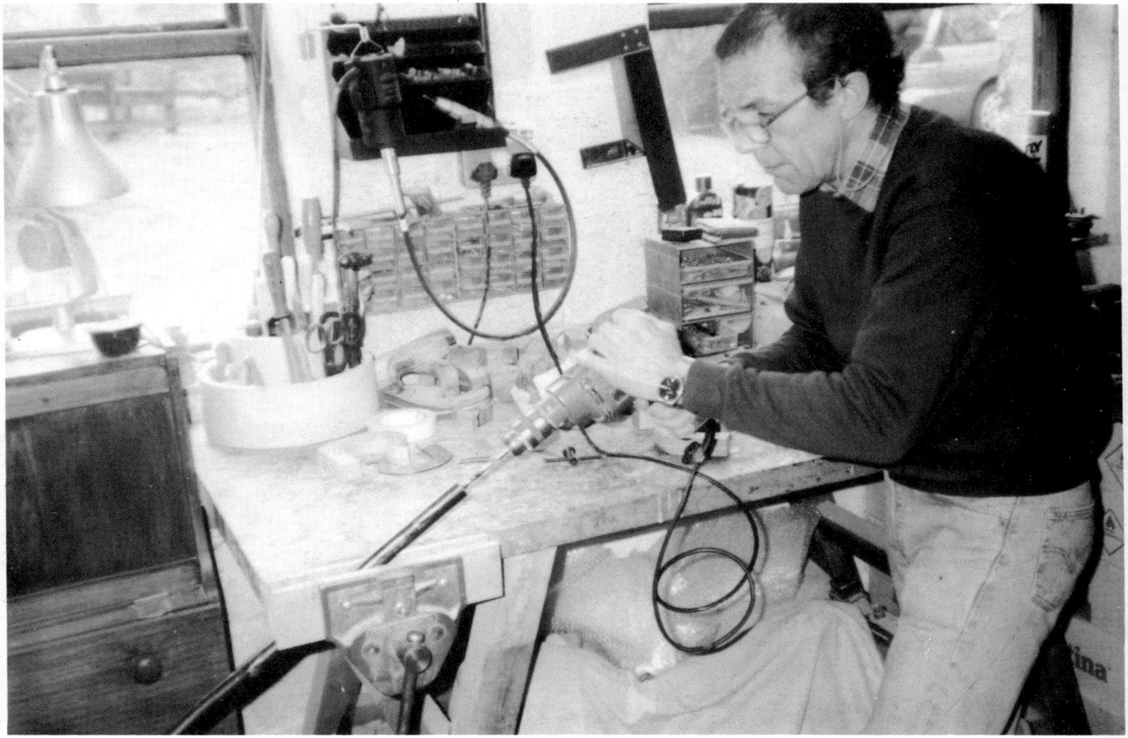

Drilling the hole in the shaft to take the other end of the pin.

Measuring the metal pin to the correct length.

Cutting the metal pin before securing it into the shaft with adhesive. Then it is allowed to dry.

Fitting the shaft and handle together.

Using adhesive to secure the handle on to the pin in the shaft.

Using masking tape to make sure the joint is tight whilst the adhesive sets.

When dry, the final whittling down of the handle is done so that the the shaft and handle are roughly the same size.

Filing down the handle to remove any major blemishes.

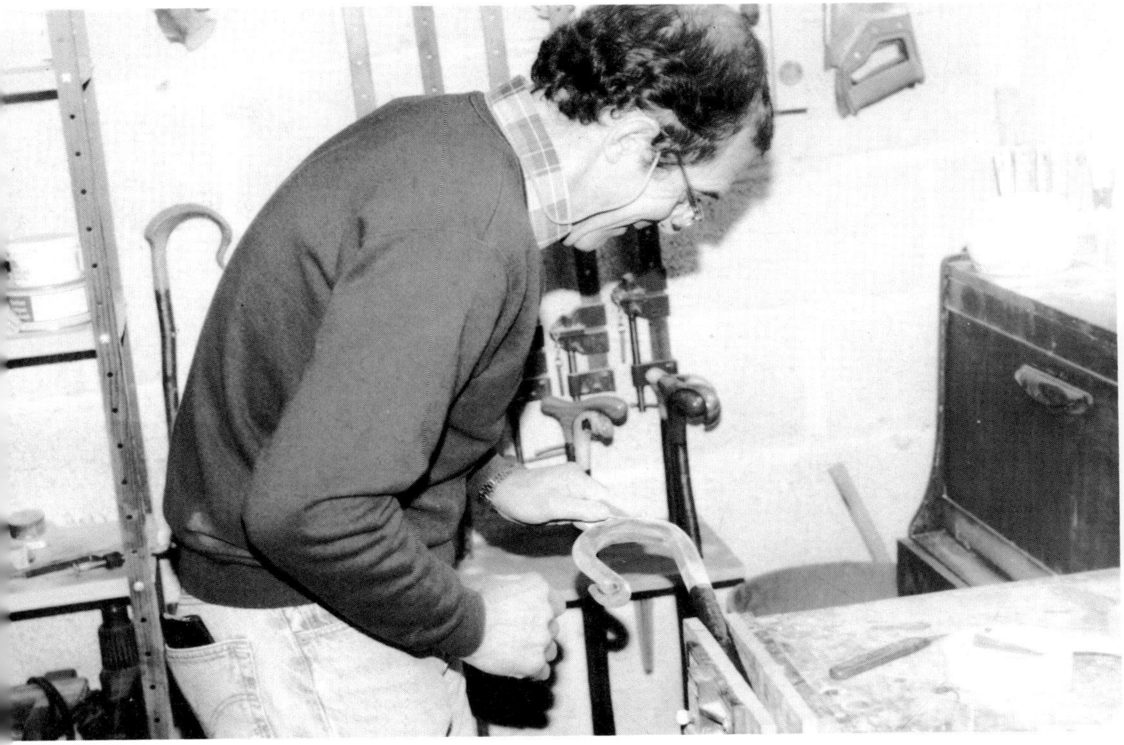

Checking for smoothness.

If any minor blemishes are found, a fine sandpaper is used to get a smooth finish.

Continue with finer sand-paper until there is a perfect finish all around the length of the handle.

Finally, give the first of several coats of polish or varnish.

The finished effect.

When using horn for the handle, first cut to the approximate shape with a bandsaw. Cut only the thick end.

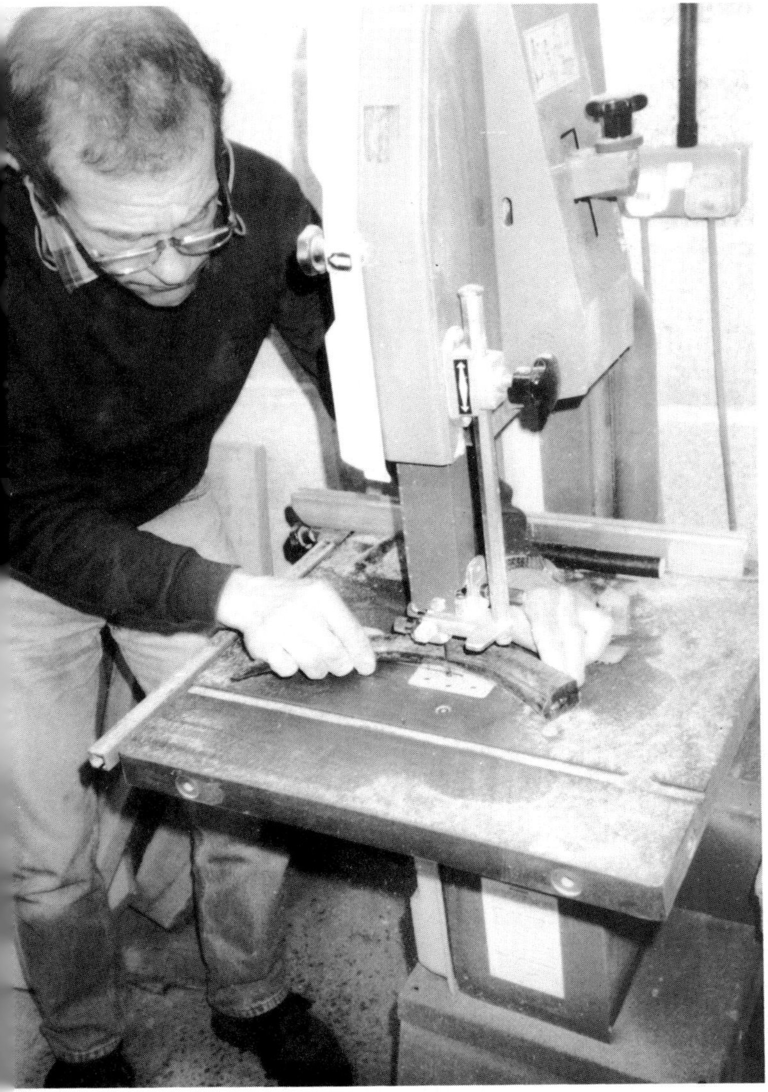

Take this cutting very slowly as horn can shatter.

For bending horn to the correct shape, use a jig. This one was specially made for Brian by the local blacksmith.

Place the thick end of the horn into the jig and secure it, in this case by tightening the screws.

Starting at the thick end, heat slowly with a hot-air gun. The horn becomes more pliable as it gets hotter. Don't worry about any charring, as this is filed down later.

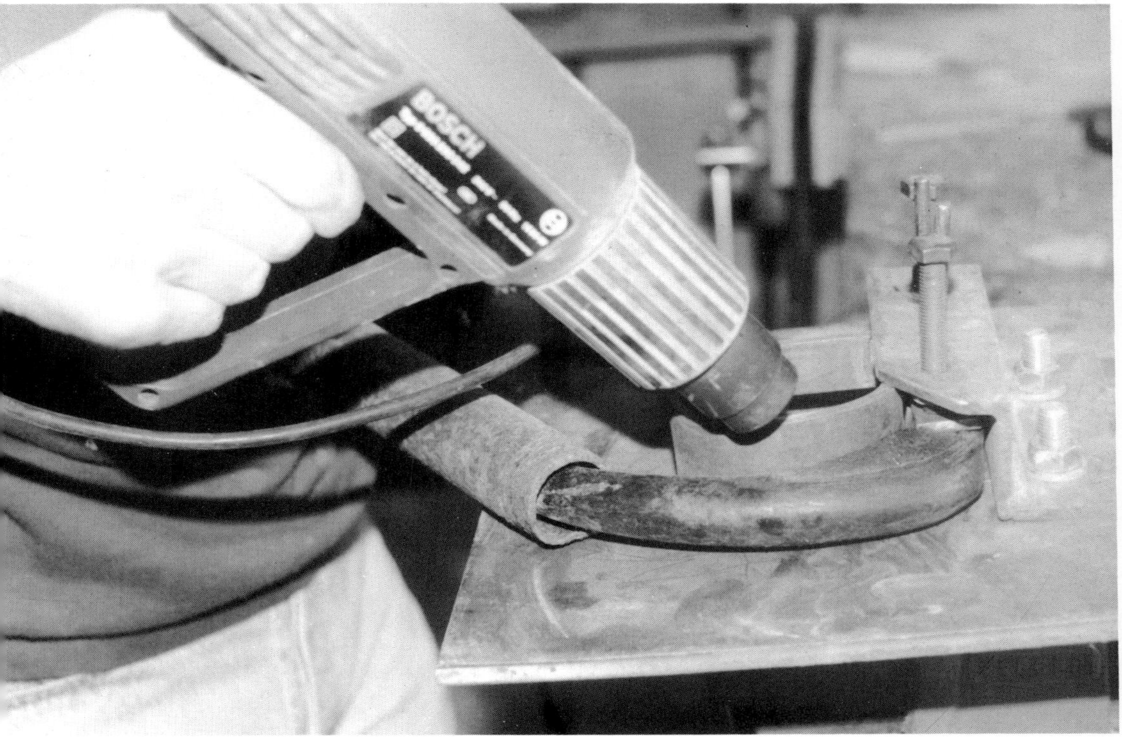

As the horn gets hotter, slowly bend it around the jig.

Secure the horn as it is bent. When it is bent along its entire length, leave it in the jig to get cold.

Brian Bannister proudly displaying the shepherd's crook that he made in the previous pages.

(Left) Three shepherd's crooks. The one on the left is made of buffalo horn.
(Right) A *leg cleek* on the left and the more usual shepherd's crook on the right.

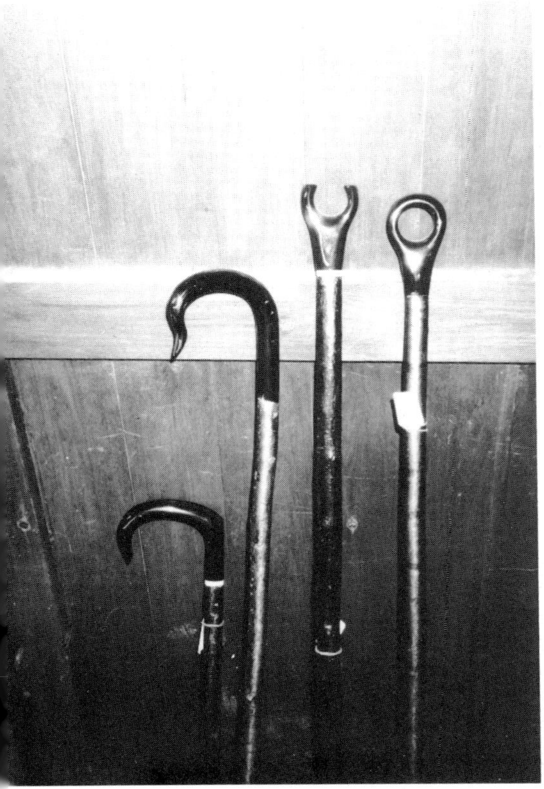

(Left) A selection of buffalo-horn sticks.
(Right) Two walking sticks made with antler horn.